CONTENTS

Searching	3
Preface	5
The First Mountain	6
Shiva	7
Boy	9
Young Man	10
Family Man	12
Purpose Work	14
Becoming an Entrepreneur	16
Expat	17
The Second Mountain	19
The Search for Spirituality	22
Zen	23
Zen Redux	24
Lila	26
Flow	28
Science	29
Rivers	33
The Dalai Lama	34
The Dark Side	36

Ready	38
Refinements	39
The Four Agreements	40
Authentic Happiness	42
Living with the End in Mind	44
Prepared	46
The Encore Years	47
Japan	48
Pilgrims	49
Ikigai	52
Grandparents	53
Ikigai and My Encore Years	54
Looking Forward	58
Appendix	60
Photographs	61
Acknowledgments	71
Bibliography	73
Other Readings	75
Exercises	76

(Cover: 2023, Kumano Kodo, Japan)

SEARCHING

Stephen Gallant

© 2025 – Stephen Gallant - All Rights Reserved

*To Melissa,
Danielle, Brendan,
Madison, Brendan,
Cameron, Jackson, Colin,
and future grandchildren*

PREFACE

I wanted to document my search for meaning and purpose in life. Of all the topics my mind ventured, this is where my mind lingered most.

I wrote this book for my children and their children. I want them to know this part of me, as I really didn't discuss. Metaphysics was far from regular life topics, and too deep, for everyday discussion. Of course, the grandchildren are too young. Whatever the reason, I felt at some point both might be interested in my thoughts. For the little ones, this may be great to have when I'm long gone.

I also wanted to share this part of me with my friends, many of whom engaged in these topics.

If nothing else, writing this book gave me joy.

Stephen Gallant
Charleston, SC
February 2025

THE FIRST MOUNTAIN

SHIVA

I worked in a world where making money was the goal. Traders and portfolio managers could measure their net worth every day. This led to a mental heuristic that dominated your goals.

I made good money. I had the big house, a great education for my children, nice cars, great trips, and more. But over the decades, making money wasn't my primary goal, even when I wanted lots of it. Sure, I was attracted to the lifestyle, status, and power. But there was something else, something that distracted that focus. As David Brooks states in the Second Mountain, "When the panther comes, it seizes you by the neck and drags you down into a dark valley. You didn't choose to go there, but now you're stuck. There's no way out, but through."

That panther always dragged me to the feet of Shiva.

Shiva is one of the principal deities in Hinduism. He is known as the "Destroyer" or "Transformer". A prominent feature is Shiva's third eye. It symbolizes divine wisdom, the ability to see beyond ordinary perception, and the ability to destroy illusion. When Shiva's third eye is closed, he maintains balance and harmony in the cosmos, embodying the role of a meditative ascetic. When his third eye is open, he unleashes a fiery energy capable of annihilating evil, ignorance, and any force that disrupt cosmic order. The eye opening represents transformative destruction, paving the way for renewal and spiritual awakening.

Shiva's eye opened for me in late 2007, and by April 2008 the transformative disruption began. Four years later, and a failed first attempt, I found professional and personal renewal. Shiva had closed his third eye. My transformation was happening. I no longer conformed to other's view of how my life should be.

But it took a long time to get to this place.

BOY

I was born into a New York Jewish American family that went through the motions of being Jewish. Like most reform Jews in the US, my family went to temple only on the high holy days, Rosh Hashanah and Yom Kippur.

I hated going to services, sitting through hours of prayers in Hebrew. My only solace in sitting patiently was the knowledge that at some point I had to go to the bathroom. There was a tacit understanding between me and my parents that once I got permission to go, I never had to return to the service.

My reward for sitting in temple was play time in front of the Hebrew school. Other kids had the same tacit agreements. The parents were probably happy to not have fidgety kids by their side while they were atoning for their sins.

For my Bar Mitzvah, I learned how to read and write Hebrew. But I learned how to read and write the sounds of the language without ever learning what the words meant. In other words, the language never spoke to me. Since the house of God didn't speak my language, I was left without any understanding and feeling for Jewish spirituality.

As I grew older, I shunned Judaism. I felt more comfortable receding into the patchwork of a secular society. It was easier to blend in and hide.

YOUNG MAN

Despite distancing myself from Judaism, I hated and feared antisemitism. As a child my fear was for my physical safety. As I grew older, I shifted my focus to questioning prejudice. I couldn't understand how someone could label me without knowing me.

Growing up in the 70's was fun. I did some crazy things. I was a rebel. My parents gave me lots of latitude. That independence allowed me to goof off, but more importantly, it helped me develop self-confidence and character.

I coasted in high school. I developed poor academic habits. I didn't take notes, I rushed through homework, and I didn't study for tests. I hated reading too. I succeeded at my minimal level of capacity. But with a little luck things came together. I got into Washington University in St. Louis, following my sister, Debbie. I think being a legacy mattered. Deb was a good student. She may have saved me.

Wash U. made a permanent, positive impact on my life. I was surrounded by great, talented people. I hit it off quickly with a great group of guys. Most of us joined Sigma Chi Fraternity. These guys were excellent students and even better partiers. They became lifelong friends.

I blossomed in college. I gravitated to leadership roles, becoming the president of my fraternity and getting appointed to Thurtene, an honorary society. My self-esteem soared.

In 1982, the US was coming out of a bad recession. It was hard to get a job. I got two job offers. I chose to work for The Northern Trust Company in Chicago. They hired me into their Management Development Program.

I loved Chicago. I loved being on my own. My days consisted of rotating through all aspects of banking, working out at the East Bank Club, and hanging out in Lincoln Park. I had a good friend who introduced me to all his friends, providing instant community. I was set.

Shiva visited me for the first time in Chicago. I didn't know it then, but when Shiva opens his eye, Shiva does what Shiva wants. There's no escaping his gaze.

Shiva's eye focused on my spiritual angst. My Jewish faith was dead. Shiva saw this disconnect and put a spotlight on it. Now it was clear: I had a deep yearning for spirituality, but I had no way of developing it. With a curious, open mind, I started to search for answers.

I searched for meaning in my life, purpose in society, and concepts that could leave me in awe. It was a confusing and contorted path. I moved from wanting to believe in God and belong to a tribe, to questioning God, to becoming comfortable with atheism. What I ultimately realized was the venue didn't matter. Spirituality was everywhere.

FAMILY MAN

I left Chicago after a year. The bank was a dead end for finding passion and purpose. I move back to New York to continue my journey.

Living in New York was not for me. I hated the rat race, and I hated the lack of nature. I spent a year trying to find passion and purpose in two separate endeavors: commercial real estate and advertising. I hated both. I was unhappy doing that work, in that culture, in that environment.

In 1984 a college friend was getting married in St. Louis. I took advantage of my trip to St. Louis by applying for a job at an investment firm I interned during college. The job was a junior bond trader. I got hired. I moved to St. Louis that same year and quickly found happiness. I loved the investment business. I loved being a trader. The bond trading business was rapidly evolving, and I was well positioned for the changes.

When I began, the fixed income market was staffed by guys who were adept at buying on the bid side and selling on the ask side, or simply, they were good at making markets. These traders achieved success with hustle, moxie, and personality. They were real characters. But by 1990, armed with computers, the best traders were the smart guys. They edged out the characters.

I gravitated to what the smart guys were doing. The smart guys quickly found a home in analytical trading instead of flow trading. Flow traders needed to know people. They needed to get the call to buy or sell something. Analytical traders needed to discern value and then make a case to sell it for more. Analytical trades meant that the price was not well understood. I was asked to lead my firm's efforts to make markets in CMOs. I built this business from scratch. I was successful. I was recognized. I was building my career.

In 1985 I met Melissa, and a year later we married. For the next 11 years St. Louis was the perfect life. Melissa and I bought our first home, and in 1988 we had our first daughter, Danielle. Three years later and a larger house, we had our second daughter, Madison.

In 1997, at 37 years old, I felt that tug again — the angst — but this time it was professional angst. I knew I could hang with the big boys on Wall Street, but I wasn't doing the most sophisticated work. I wanted to be closer to the leading edge of my field. Luckily, serendipity happened. My favorite client, ING, asked me to work for them. ING Americas was a large, sophisticated, institutional investor. We moved to Atlanta, Georgia, where ING Americas had their headquarters.

I loved the portfolio management business. Trading was about the next trade, but portfolio management was about the whole process: investing, managing performance, managing risk, accounting, managing people, and interfacing with a wide variety of internal and external folks. For the next 11 years, I was happy.

But in 2008, Shiva opened his third eye again.

PURPOSE WORK

Work became bureaucratic. I spent my time sitting in meetings. I was 47 years old, facing the decision to hunker down until retirement, or take a risk. I knew that if I didn't tap into my sense of passion and purpose, I would have to face my greatest fear, living a life of quiet desperation. I quit cold.

The first thing I did was attend a workshop in California with my close friend and ING colleague, Greg. This workshop was a weeklong program designed to help one uncover their purpose. Greg and I were fortunate. We were the only ones attending this week. It was a very personal experience.

Through a series of meditations, discussions, interviews, and journalling, certain words, phrases, and ideas arose. I would unpackage these thoughts to the seminar leaders. They discerned if these thoughts were authentic – signs of my truest self — or if they were inauthentic — signs that I was grandstanding, ego-boosting, or self-promoting.

In writing this book I went through my journals from this seminar. The work centered on defining three things: 1) my essence, 2) my blessing, and 3) my mission. These three are similar to defining your ikigai, which I write about later. Your essence is your passion, your blessing is something you're good at, and your mission is taking your essence and your blessing into the world, where it's needed. Let's use an example. If my passion was Jiu Jitsu then my essence and mission could be teaching Jiu Jitsu.

My essence involved beauty. This was somewhat difficult because my verb was challenging. What was my skill I was performing? It didn't help when I refined my essence to "live amidst beauty". From skiing, to flyfishing, to traveling, to where we lived, they all led with beauty. But how was that my purpose?

I worked on it some more. Finally, my mission evolved to being an advocate, steward, and active participant in the world's beauty: an Ambassador for Beauty. This was me. I was always going to places of beauty with others – like the Galapagos, or Cappadocia, or the Kumano. Each time, I lead with passion. It truly was my gift.

What is beauty to me? Beauty to me is very broad. I see beauty in nature, in people, in culture, in a business plan, and even in a programmed algorithm. Beauty is all around me. In looking for this definition I came across a power statement from that seminar. A power statement is a concise, compelling, declaration that reinforces confidence, purpose, and direction. It serves as a mental anchor to help you stay focused and motivated:

"Wherever I look I see beauty, and my curiosity drives me to create new ways to appreciate that beauty and help others appreciate it as well."

BECOMING AN ENTREPRENEUR

At ING I had a front row seat to the Great Financial Crisis of 2008. It was obvious from where I sat that ING, a prominent Dutch financial services company with operations around the world, had to reassure the world that they were safe. I thought, "I'm going to be a high paid babysitter for these portfolios". I knew the Dutch leadership would put a moratorium on investing in my asset classes, and with that, I wouldn't be able to take advantage of my skills. So, with Shiva in the background, and then the crisis, I knew I needed to go out on my own.

I first thought I could simply trade on my own. While I had a modicum of success sitting at my computer and trading at home, it was terribly unfulfilling. There were no people to interact with, no teams to develop, no culture to create.

EXPAT

I decided to search for an idea. I wanted to build a company. I wanted to use my investment skills, but now I also wanted to make an impact. Through my search, I chose to start a company that would invest in technologies that could improve water quality or water quantity. I found Adam, a subject matter expert, and we agreed to partner together. We developed the firm and pitched it to top strategic investors all over the US. But with the GFC wounds still sore, no one was willing to take new risks. Adam and I decided it was best for our careers, and our family's well-being, to shutter the company and move on.

With a little luck, I pivoted myself towards another new idea: starting an offshore reinsurance company. This idea developed nicely, and it got financially backed. We decided to build the company in Switzerland for tax and regulatory purposes. I raised my hand, along with another partner, to move there. In 2013, we moved to Zürich and successfully launched Weisshorn Reinsurance AG (later, renamed Somerset Reinsurance Ltd). We also launched our Bermuda operation with two other partners. I led many aspects of the startup. I built the investment and risk process, championed a novel system architecture, developed governance processes, helped lead the regulatory and rating agency process, built teams, and more.

Our life in Zürich was fantastic. For the first time in my life I was living a life of true passion: I was a successful entrepreneur, I was building something of lasting value, and I was nurturing talent into a high performing team. I was on fire with all of it. I also was living in my kind of temple, the Swiss Alps. The Alps were a dream. I could ski, hike, and be in awe.

For five years I was content. My spirit was soaring. But while I was happy with the life Melissa and I were living, we were far from our children. Our children were independent and living their lives successfully back home. But Melissa and I weren't there. This seemed to work until Danielle had a child.

Moving back to the US awakened Shiva again. Shiva's all-knowing power recognized that my spiritual journey was far from complete, and it was time for me to become a searcher again.

I read many impactful works up to this point. These works gave me principles to live my life. They were metaphysical and philosophical ideologies. They were tools for my introspective work. They were the path to my spirituality. I needed to revisit them now and add additional works to the mix. What follows are the works that made the biggest impact on me.

THE SECOND MOUNTAIN

In The Second Mountain, the author, David Brooks explains:

"Life isn't one mountain — it's two. The First Mountain is what the world tells you to climb: success, achievement, recognition. It's about building yourself up, staking your claim, proving you belong. But at the top, something feels off. The air is thin, the view hollow. That's when the second mountain appears. It's not about you anymore. It's about others. It's about commitment — to relationships, to a calling, to something bigger than yourself. The Second Mountain isn't climbed alone; it's climbed with love, service, and humility as your guides."

Brooks argues that the Second Mountain shifts the center of gravity in life. He notes that one stops asking, "What can I get?" and instead begins to ask, "What can I give?" In this framework, joy replaces happiness, depth replaces breadth, and purpose takes the place of ambition.

While Brooks acknowledges that this climb is not easy, he asserts it is far more meaningful. According to Brooks, the Second Mountain isn't about reaching the top; rather, it's about being transformed by the journey itself. He emphasizes leaving behind the ego of the First Mountain and stepping into the life one is truly meant to live. "That's where the real view is," Brooks concludes.

My Second Mountain was daunting — far more so than my First Mountain. Society, as Brooks observes, prepares us for the First Mountain as though it's the only one that matters. From the very start, we are taught to climb — get the grades, build the resume, and chase the promotion. It's a relentless pursuit of achievement, meant to prove one's worth in a system that measures everything by success. Schools train us for the competition, businesses reward the hustle, and culture sells us a story that happiness is something to be earned — something to be conquered. But the climb, as Brooks illustrates, often leaves a void. Reaching the top of the First Mountain feels incomplete. Something vital is missing.

The issue, Brooks argues, isn't with the climb itself; it's with the mountain. The First Mountain is rooted in the self: one's career, goals, and recognition. It is a world of doing, without much thought for being. Beyond this, however, Brooks posits that a Second Mountain awaits. Unlike the First, the Second Mountain is not about chasing but about giving. The world does not prepare us for this shift, because the Second Mountain isn't something you are trained to climb; it is something you stumble upon when the First Mountain no longer satisfies. According to Brooks, it is in this moment of transition that life begins to make sense.

Getting to the top of the First Mountain took most of my life. But now I was at the starting line again. I was facing questions like "What now?" I had no choice but to get comfortable with this new chapter. I had to come down from the First Mountain, and walk away from the status, power, and wealth. I had to venture into a Wilderness — for a long time — to find my way to my Second Mountain. I learned that the tools of the First Mountain were of no help. They were useless and had to be set aside. Finding my Second Mountain required new skills to be developed.

I spent my adult life on a quest for spirituality through an understanding of metaphysics, or the fundamental nature of reality, existence, and being. I did this through reading books by great authors. Their works shaped me. They helped me confidently venture into the Wilderness between my First and Second Mountains.

THE SEARCH FOR SPIRITUALITY

ZEN

I once delved into the writings of D.T. Suzuki, the western world's foremost guide to understanding Zen Buddhism.

D.T. Suzuki introduced Zen Buddhism to the Western world by emphasizing its experiential, non-dogmatic nature, focusing on direct insight and personal experience over intellectual understanding or ritual practice. He highlighted Zen as a path to awakening that transcends traditional logic, using paradoxical koans and practices like meditation to cultivate a state of "no-mind" (mushin) and deep intuitive awareness. Suzuki framed Zen as a universal spiritual approach that could resonate with Western audiences, often linking its teachings to Western philosophy, psychology, and art, thereby presenting Zen as not just a religion but a profound way of living and perceiving reality.

ZEN REDUX

From there, I discovered one of my two favorite authors, Robert Pirsig. His famous first book, Zen and the Art of Motorcycle Maintenance made a big impact. Pirsig was a fountain of insights that really started me on my spiritual path.

A central tenet of the book focused on The Hierarchy of Quality (with a capital "Q"). Quality begins at the base, where it's raw and undefined — felt, not thought. It's the immediate experience, the moment before you name it or analyze it. This is the foundation, where everything starts. Above that is the romantic level, where Quality takes on emotion and beauty. It's the sparkle in a freshly polished chrome, the feeling of freedom on the open road. Romantic understanding is intuitive, focused on the surface and the moment.

Then comes the classical level, where Quality shifts from feeling to reason. Here, it's about structure, precision, and understanding the mechanics beneath the surface. It's not just about how something looks but how it works, how the parts come together to make a whole. Classical understanding digs deeper, into the nuts and bolts of reality.

But the hierarchy isn't complete until these two — romantic and classical — merge. The highest level of Quality is their integration, a harmony where intuition and reason coexist. It's not one over the other; it's both, balanced and complete. This is where life starts to feel whole, where the machine hums perfectly, and the road stretches endlessly ahead.

The alluring thing for me was the allegory of the whole book, where the journey on the open road is a metaphor for life. The road rolls out ahead of you, endless, but the ride is never about the end. It's about what happens between here and there. You twist the throttle, feel the hum of the engine, and suddenly you're not just riding — you're part of the road.

I never meditated before — I didn't know how. Once I started, I learned that I had to pay attention to what I was doing and how I was feeling. I became fully present, fully alive. It wasn't some mystical state. I was just being. When you're present, you stop fighting time. You just flow with it.

LILA

I was excited to read Pirsig's next and final book, Lila: An Inquiry into Morals. Pirsig improved on the Hierarchy of Quality with the Hierarchy of Morals. Morals, Pirsig says, aren't carved in stone — they're alive, evolving, built layer by layer like the structure of life itself. At the base is biological morality, the instinct to survive, to eat, to reproduce. Above that is social morality, where the survival of the group takes precedence over the individual. It's where laws, traditions, and cultures grow, holding life together with the glue of shared values. Then comes intellectual morality, breaking free from the confines of tradition. This is the realm of ideas, reason, and the freedom to question.

But at the top is dynamic Quality, the spark that breaks all the rules. It's what moves life forward, destroying the old to make room for the new. These levels aren't in conflict — they're in balance — a hierarchy of value where each supports the other. Without the base, the higher levels crumble. Without the higher levels, life stagnates.

True morality isn't about choosing one level over another — it's about finding harmony in the whole, letting each level serve its purpose without strangling the others. That's the heart of it: a living, breathing morality tuned to the rhythm of Quality.

Pirsig's work raised questions in my mind. Questions are dangerous things. They poke holes in the comfortable fabric of what you think you know. But they're also necessary. They open up space for something new, something better. When I started asking the big questions, "What is Quality? What is life? Who am I?", I didn't always get answers. But what I did get was something more important: clarity. It's not about finding the truth; it's about living with it. That's where growth happens — in the asking, not the answering.

This thought emerged in my corporate career. My executive coach, Andy, shared words from a plaque above his desk. It was a quote from Letters to a Young Poet, by Ranier Rilke:

Be patient towards all that is unsolved in your heart and try to love the questions themselves. Do not seek the answers, which cannot be given because you would not be able to live with them and the point is to live everything. Live the questions now. Perhaps you will gradually, without noticing it, live along some distant day into the answer.

FLOW

As a young boy I loved NASTAR slalom racing. I loved the rhythm of the turns, with its cadence that beat like a song. Skiing with my boots clicking together, quickly turning through the bumps, I experienced a sense of flow. I was making music, turning to the sound of "da-daa, da-daa, da-daa". I gave control of my skis to the process, and the skis just moved.

A friend recommended a book called, Flow: The Psychology of Optimal Experience by Mihaly Csikszentmihalyi. It explained what I was feeling when I skied.

Flow is that rare state where everything clicks. You lose track of time, and the work becomes its own reward. It's not about success or failure; it's about being so completely absorbed in what you're doing that the rest of the world falls away. I knew that feeling: It was like a perfect day skiing through fresh pow pow.

Mihaly Csikszentmihalyi called it optimal experience, but it's more than that — its life lived fully in the moment. There's no separation between you and the task. It's as if the boundary between subject and object disappears, leaving only pure engagement.

The key to flow is balance. The challenge must meet your skill. Too easy, and you're bored. Too hard, and you're frustrated. But when they align, there's harmony — a rhythm you step into, where action and awareness merge. Flow isn't something you chase; it's something you allow. When it happens, you're not just doing — you're being. And in that being, life suddenly makes sense.

SCIENCE

My mental model for how I was going to live life was coming into view, but I needed more to get to my Second Mountain. I needed to be fully aware and be completely present. I needed to make space for something new, something better. I knew experiencing flow was the truest form of being. But I needed a Hierarchy of Quality to put things in their rightful place.

My older, wiser self was being patient with all that was unsolved. I was living with my questions, like, "What do you believe?", "What's the root of your belief?", and "Why is this belief important?"

Up until this point I had no experience in science or scientific process. Luckily, my passion for investing led me to the field of biotech, which made a case for me to learn about biochemistry and genetics. These fields provided fundamental properties in the human condition, and consequentially, led me to a place of awe.

Alleles

The Social Conquest of Earth was written by E.O. Wilson, a brilliant American professor who specialized in the social biology of ants, and more generally, eusocial creatures, like humans. Wilson explained people better than anyone else.

Wilson's premise starts with alleles, a variant form of a gene that occupies a specific position on a chromosome. Different alleles can result in variations in traits, or phenotypes, such as eye color or blood type. They are bits of genetic code, swapping and competing over millennia, building human life as we know it.

Wilson broadens the view by saying alleles didn't just create bodies — they created societies, shaping instincts, emotions, and the capacity for culture. Wilson's point here is humans aren't just the product of individual selection, clawing for survival. We're shaped by group selection too, where teamwork and altruism became as essential as strength and cunning. The tension between these forces — the selfish gene and the cooperative group — is where humanity emerged. It's not a story of perfection but of process, that worked itself out over billions of years. Alleles set the foundation, but the structure — the art of being human — is something we built together.

With alleles firmly planted as the foundation to many answers to questions like, "Why are we here" and "How did we evolve", I moved away from the concept of God and towards the world of science. If science had an answer, great. If a topic remained beyond what science knew, that was fine too. I did not invoke the God of the Gaps, or the tendency to fill gaps in scientific knowledge with supernatural explanations, which often recede as scientific understanding advances.

Biochemistry

Investing in biotech required a practical understanding of chemistry and atomic physics. In the world of atoms, there's a kind of quiet, almost philosophical negotiation taking place — a push and pull between greed and generosity. Some elements, like oxygen, hold their electrons close, tight-fisted like a miser guarding treasure, while others, like sodium, are more like a wanderer shedding what they don't need. It's not morality but necessity that drives them. Electrons, with their restless energy, dance between these poles of possessiveness and sharing. Covalent bonds are formed not out of altruism but a mutual agreement — a shared existence where neither atom loses and both gain. Ionic bonds, on the other hand, are more like a power play: one atom seizes what it craves while the other acquiesces, finding stability in surrender. The balance of life itself rests on this atomic interplay, an unseen world of give and take, where even the smallest particles wrestle with the paradox of holding on and letting go.

From this delicate dance of electrons, this endless negotiation of give and take, life emerges — not as some grand, sudden event but as the inevitable poetry of balance. Carbon, that quiet architect, steps forward, not with dominance but with versatility, extending its hand in all directions, forming chains, rings, and scaffolds that can hold the complexity of life itself. Water, too, plays its part, a molecule born of sharing and yet capable of pulling others into its orbit, dissolving, connecting, catalyzing. These molecules, these seemingly inert particles, do not intend to create life — they simply follow their nature, their tendency toward stability, and in doing so, create a foundation for something larger than themselves. Out of the chaos of chemistry arises the order of biology, the whispered truth that the universe, through its own laws, seeks not just survival but complexity, beauty, and, perhaps, understanding.

This process, so intricate yet so unassuming, doesn't need the weight of divine intervention to justify its elegance. It doesn't demand faith, only observation — only the quiet awe of seeing how the smallest, simplest interactions can build toward something profound. There's no need for commandments or miracles when the rules of the universe, written in the language of electrons and energy, already hold the answers. The beauty here isn't diminished by its lack of intent; it's amplified. Life isn't a gift handed down, but a masterpiece painted by chance and physics, by the natural tendencies of the universe itself. And in that, there's a deeper kind of wonder.

Einstein

One of my heroes is Albert Einsten [1]. He believed God was rooted in awe and reverence for the harmony and order of the universe, rather than belief in a personal deity who intervenes in human affairs. He famously aligned with Spinoza's God, a divine essence manifest in the laws of nature and the unity of existence, not in religious dogma or rituals. For Einstein, this "cosmic religious sense" wasn't about worship but about humility and curiosity in the face of life's infinite complexity. He saw science and spirituality as complementary paths to understanding the eternal mystery, with the divine as the binding principle of all things rather than a figure of human projection.

❋ ❋ ❋

---

[1] I have five heroes: 1) Albert Einstein - Trait: Brilliance. Modern words could not explain what he figured out. 2) Auguste Rodin - Trait: Artistic Visionary. Groundbreaking beauty in sculpture. Stood up to the establishment for his art. 3) Ralph Waldo Emerson - Trait: Original Thinker. Wrote Self Reliance. 4) Earnest Shackleton - Trait: Leadership. Greatest story of survival. Saved his entire expedition. 5) Abraham Gallant (my great grandfather) - Trait: Community. He "wore the crown of Torah".

RIVERS

I am passionate about flyfishing. Flyfishing is both a refuge and a metaphor for navigating life's complexities. The art of casting, the patience of waiting, and the intimate connection with nature all fit into that complexity, as an analogy for life.

In my favorite novel, The River Why, the author David James Duncan explains the pursuit more spiritually, as the protagonist's pursuit of individual mastery gives way to a deeper, more fluid understanding of life. Duncan echoes a Zen-like sensibility: the idea that true wisdom comes not from dominating life, but from being immersed in its current, its flow, attuned to its harmonies.

The river becomes not just a place but a teacher, where fulfillment lies not in achieving perfection but in surrendering to life's mysteries. It's a call to live fully in the present, to appreciate the sacred in the ordinary, and to embrace the ineffable beauty of being a small part of something vast and eternal.

THE DALAI LAMA

Back in 2020 my best friend Gib was diagnosed with a rare and aggressive form of non-Hodgkins's lymphoma. I rearranged my schedule to visit Gib in the hospital every day. I needed to be present for both of us.

At one point during the cancer treatment Gib mentioned that he was reading The Art of Happiness, by the Dalai Lama. Gib found solace from the Dalai Lama's words. Gib paraphrased him, saying, "Lucky is the man who can identify and deal with all his devils and his angels, and then adapt his life to deal with them all."

This idea of happiness, from a close friend at risk of dying, moved me deeply. Gib recovered. I bought the book.

Happiness, the Dalai Lama argues, is not an external object to be chased but a state of mind cultivated from within. It is a discipline, a practice, and ultimately a choice. He states, "The purpose of our life is to seek happiness". But this isn't the fleeting happiness found in material pleasures or momentary victories. It is a deeper, more enduring sense of well-being, born of inner peace and compassion for others. This kind of happiness is not passive — it demands active effort and a willingness to confront the turbulence of the human condition. At the heart of his teaching is the idea that suffering, though unavoidable, is not absolute. It's how we respond to suffering that shapes our happiness. "If you want others to be happy, practice compassion. If you want to be happy, practice compassion." Compassion, then, is not just an altruistic ideal but a practical tool, a means of dissolving the boundaries between self and other. It is a way of aligning the mind with the natural order of human connection. In practicing compassion, we escape the narrow confines of ego and see ourselves as part of a greater whole.

But cultivating happiness, as he describes, requires discipline over the mind itself. "The systematic training of the mind — the cultivation of happiness, the genuine inner transformation by deliberately selecting and focusing on positive mental states and challenging negative mental states — is possible because of the very structure and function of the brain." It's a reminder that happiness isn't accidental or gifted; it is earned through mindfulness, reflection, and persistence.

The Dalai Lama's insights, though rooted in Buddhism, invite each person to examine their own lives, their own values, and to take responsibility for their own happiness. They also remind us about not escaping the chaos of life but finding harmony within it.

THE DARK SIDE

Greg recommended I read The Dark Side of the Light Chasers, by Debbie Ford. It was an important book. It's two-hundred pages were full of insights and wisdom. It took me ten months to read: at the end of each chapter were exercises, and those exercises, if you did them honestly, required a lot of work on yourself.

The purpose of the book is to help one reconcile their light side and their dark side. To do that, one must first abandon the illusion that light is good and dark is bad. That's the first trap, the most insidious one, because the light side masquerades as virtue. People want to be good. They want to be kind, successful, admired. They craft identities around these virtues, polishing them like well-kept machinery, until they gleam so brightly that the shadows lurking beneath them — the dark side — are ignored — banished to some forgotten chamber in the mind. But ignored isn't erased. The shadows don't go anywhere. They just bide their time.

The real work begins when you stop running from the dark side, or the parts of yourself that don't fit the image you've created. It's uncomfortable, because you find what has always been there — anger, envy, selfishness, weakness. The pieces that don't match your ideal self. Ford suggests that these disowned parts are not just obstacles to be overcome but lost aspects of your wholeness. You don't transcend them by force. You listen to them. You make peace with them. You recognize that the same energy that fuels impatience also fuels drive. The same force behind arrogance also powers confidence. There is no rejecting one without diminishing the other.

The right answer is a synthesis, not a battle, between light and dark. It's an understanding that they are extensions of the same essence, you. It's a meticulous process, neither suppressing nor overindulging any single piece. In the end, the goal isn't to become some perfected being of pure light, nor is it to revel in the dark. It's to be whole. To know yourself so completely that nothing within you remains unclaimed. The dark and the light work together, not against each other. And when that happens, you just are.

READY

These works all describe a union of two seemingly opposing concepts: Suzuki's no-mind and awareness, Csikszentmihalyi's disappearing boundary between subject and object, Pirsig's dynamic Quality, where romantic morality and intellectual morality co-exist, Wilson's atoms that mutually attract and repel, the Dalai Lama's Buddhist belief that the acceptance of suffering leads to happiness, and Ford's dark and light sides working together rather than against each other.

The way of The Wilderness was no different. I had to be lost and found at the same time. And with that, I had stepped off my First Mountain.

REFINEMENTS

THE FOUR AGREEMENTS

The Four Agreements by Don Miguel Ángel Ruiz Macías isn't a book about commandments handed down from some higher authority, telling you what you must do. They're more like tuning adjustments — subtle shifts that bring your mind into alignment, stripping away the noise, the unnecessary friction that makes life feel harder than it has to be.

Be impeccable with your word

Understand that words aren't just sounds; they're tools, precision instruments capable of building or destroying. Use them carelessly, and they corrode the system, introducing rust into the gears. Use them with intention, and they refine and sharpen the machine, keeping it running smoothly.

Don't take anything personally

This is a tough one, because the ego wants to be at the center of everything. But when you stop assuming every action or insult is about you, a whole lot of unnecessary suffering just drops away.

Don't make assumptions

Assumptions are just shortcuts the mind takes when it's too impatient to wait for the full picture. They lead to misunderstandings, conflicts, and the kind of entropy that breaks *down relationships.*

Always do your best

This isn't some motivational platitude. It's an acknowledgment that your "best" isn't fixed — it fluctuates, shifting with your energy, your health, your circumstances. But if you're always giving what you have in that moment, there's nothing left to regret.

Practicing these agreements sounds simple, but its anything but simple. The mind resists change like an old bolt that's rusted into place. From the moment we're born, we inherit a system of thinking built on assumptions, personal reactions, and careless words. Society conditions us to take things personally, to form judgments before we have the full story, to wield language recklessly. Unlearning all of that takes work. It's not about perfection — it's about constant adjustment, refining the process, noticing when you're slipping into old patterns and making the necessary corrections. And maybe, after enough repetition, it becomes second nature.

AUTHENTIC HAPPINESS

I once attended a management development program in The Netherlands. A lecturer, a professor from Trinity University, highlighted concepts from Authentic Happiness, a book about positive psychology written by Martin Seligman. As I was interested in these concepts the professor encouraged me to explore this book further.

At the heart of Authentic Happiness lies the concept of signature strengths. Signature strengths are not just tools for success; they are the essence of who you are when you're at your best. They are deeply ingrained traits — curiosity, kindness, perseverance, or creativity — that resonate with something intrinsic and enduring in you. When you use them, you feel alive, as though you're in perfect alignment with the world around you. But these strengths are more than skills or talents; they're a form of expression, a way of engaging with life that feels authentic, effortless, and fulfilling.

Seligman describes how living in accordance with your signature strengths creates a sense of flow — a state where action and awareness merge, where time fades and the distinction between effort and ease dissolves. "The good life," he writes, "is using your signature strengths every day to produce authentic happiness and abundant gratification." It's not about becoming something you're not; it's about uncovering what was already there, refining it, and letting it thrive in the context that matters most to you.

In Pirsig's language, signature strengths could be seen as the Quality of the self, the patterns of value that define your unique way of interacting with the world. They are not imposed or manufactured but arise naturally when you move with the grain of your own being. To live through your strengths is to engage in life, not mechanically, but harmoniously. Each action is imbued with meaning because it comes from a place of genuine connection — to yourself, to others, and to the world.

Relationships are fundamental too. Happiness is not a solitary pursuit but a shared experience. Positive emotions like gratitude and optimism thrive in connection with others. They create a kind of feedback loop where giving and receiving reinforce each other. Meaning is born in these connections where we lift others up and allow ourselves to be lifted.

Finally, Seligman states that happiness is not accidental; it's intentional. Gratitude, mindfulness, and kindness are not just practices but philosophies, ways of approaching life with openness and curiosity. In this, happiness is less a feeling and more a way of being, a state where action and awareness align, and the beauty of existence is fully realized.

LIVING WITH THE END IN MIND

I was quite moved writing and presenting my parents eulogies. I often think to myself, "Who would be at my funeral? Who would speak? What would they say?"

Living with the end in mind means seeing your life as a story that's already being written, even if you've never bothered to look at the plot. Most people don't. They wake up, do what they did yesterday, react to whatever happens, and call that 'living'. But Stephen Covey, in his book, The Seven Habits of Highly Effective People, suggests stopping for a moment — stepping outside of it all — and imagining something most people try not to: your own funeral.

Four people stand up to speak. Someone from your family, a close friend, a colleague, and someone from your community. What do they say? Not just polite eulogies, but the real stuff — who you were, what you stood for, what your presence in their life actually meant.

His message was this: If you don't like what you hear in this exercise, now is the time to change it.

That's the point. Not just existing, not just getting through the days, but shaping something intentional. Most people inherit their values the way they inherit an old watch — passed down without question. They don't ask if it's accurate, or even if it works for them. Covey's idea is to take a step back and consciously design a life that leads to the kind of legacy you want, rather than just hoping it turns out that way. It's not about rigidly mapping out every detail. It's about setting a trajectory, deciding what actually matters, and then making sure your daily actions align with it. Without that, life is just momentum — things happening, days passing, with no real sense of whether any of it was what you wanted.

PREPARED

All these ideas had a place in developing my growth. They prepared me for stepping off my First Mountain with intention, without looking back. Certain concepts, like flow or happiness, were consistently popping up now. I felt my mental model for seeking joy and spiritual tranquility was mature now. I was ready to venture into my Encore Years.

THE ENCORE YEARS

JAPAN

Having lived abroad I knew that other cultures were better for folks in the encore years. One such culture was Japan. Japan fascinates me. This fascination, born from an early age watching the mini-series Shogun, grew into a passion. I studied the Japanese language, and professionally, managed a portfolio for an ING Japan affiliate. In 2003 I travelled to Japan for the first time. It was a dream come true. I spoke a little Japanese, I rode the shinkansen, bathed in an onsen, and slept in a yukata. I went back every year to meet with my clients, and my knowledge of Japan grew.

In 2009 we took our family to Japan. I wanted to share my passion for Japan with them. This time, I ventured into the countryside. I wasn't there for work, so I could really focus on the culture. This trip increased my understanding of what the Japanese culture could offer.

PILGRIMS

In 2021, during the pandemic, my longtime friend Bill mentioned that he wanted to hike the Kumano Kodo. "What's the Kumano Kodo", I asked. "It's an ancient pilgrimage trail" he answered. I looked into it. It sounded ideal, so Melissa, me, Bill, and Joanne agreed to hike the trail. By 2023, after two pandemic-delayed itineraries, Japan opened to the world, and we were on our way.

The Kumano is a sacred area in the Kii Peninsula, historically associated with Shinto and Buddhist pilgrimage traditions. "Kumano" can be translated as "deep, mysterious place," reflecting the region's dense forests, rugged mountains, and spiritual aura.

The Kumano Kodo, or "the ancient road of Kumano". consists of five main pilgrimage routes. The Kumano Kodo leads pilgrims to the three grand shrines, or the Kumano Sanzen. We hiked the Nakahechi route, which was traditionally used by the imperial family and aristocrats traveling from Kyoto.

Our first day we started in Takahara and hiked to Chikasuyu. This section went through a profoundly serene forest, with towering cedars, flowing water, and beautiful shafts of light casting rays of sunshine. We were alone. We had the full beauty of the forest to ourselves. It was the perfect setting for our first experience on the Kumano Kodo. I was fully immersed in my sense of purpose, being amidst beauty with others.

The next day we hiked the Akagi-goe trail, which leads to Yunomine Onsen. The Akagi-goe is a historic and spiritual path. Starting from Hosshinmon-oji, the trail climbs steadily through dense forests, where wooden way markers guide you along the path. Along the way, small shrines and stone statues peek out from the undergrowth, quiet witnesses to centuries of devotion.

As you crest the ridge, the trees open to reveal sweeping views of the valley below, the distant mountains folding into one another in shades of green and blue.

The next day we walked to the first of the Kumano Sanzen, Kumano Hongu Taisha. This grand temple, or taisha, is considered the spiritual center of the Kumano region — the gateway between the earthly and the divine.

The temple was originally located on a nearby floodplain, at Oyunohara. But after a devastating flood in 1889, it was moved to its current, higher location. Today, the Oyunohara floodplain remains a sacred space, marked by the monumental Oyunohara Torii. The torii serves as a symbolic gateway to the shrine's ancient origins, reminding visitors of its enduring significance in the Kumano Kodo pilgrimage.

At Kumano Hongu Taisha, we performed a specific ritual. First, we each placed a small coin into the offering box, then we pulled on a rope that rang a bell, which is meant to purify ourselves and to call the deity's attention. Then we bowed deeply, twice. Then we clapped our hands twice to once again draw the deity's attention. Then we made a silent prayer, expressing gratitude or wishes, then we bowed deeply twice more.

The next day, we went straight to one of the most famous sections of the Kumano — The Daimonzaka.

The Daimonzaka is an impressive, cedar-lined path of moss-covered stone steps, leading up to the Kumano Nachi Taisha, the second of the Kumano Sanzen. This path serves as a spiritual prelude, symbolizing the journey from the earthy realm to the divine space of the shrine. Walking the steps is seen as an act of purification and reverence. The grand shrine is at the top, where we participated in another ritual and prayer to the gods.

The next day we went to Shingu, the end of the Kumano Kodo. Traditionally, pilgrims float down the Kumano River to get to Shingu and the final shrine of the Kumano Sanzen, Kumano Hayatama Taisha. We opted for more modern transportation.

After praying for the last time at the grand shrine, we headed to the trailhead of the Kamikura Shrine.

The Kamikura Shrine is perched high on a hill overlooking the sea, next to an incredibly large boulder. In Shinto, natural objects such as rocks, mountains, and trees can be considered sacred, and are often venerated as *yorishiro*, or objects that are capable of housing *kami*. Kami is a deity or spirit that inhabits these natural objects. This large rock, called Gotobiki-iwa, is ringed by a large rope, called a *shimenawa*. This sacred rope is made of twisted straw and hemp. The rope represents purity and acts as a barrier to keep out impurities or evil spirits, preserving the sanctity of the object.

Sitting atop the shrine, I reflected on the Kumano region. I saw it as part of a universal, natural temple — places that generate a sense of Zen, flow, morality, nature, and happiness. "Awe" is best word to describe them.

I was firmly in the Wilderness now, far from my First Mountain. The Kumano Kodo was leading me to my Second Mountain.

IKIGAI

Our local bookshop displayed a book titled Ikigai: The Japanese Secret to a Long and Happy Life, by Héctor García and Francesc Miralles. I knew about ikigai from my research on longevity and specifically, the Blue Zones. Ikigai played heavily into the long lives of Okinawans.

The authors present ikigai not as some lofty ideal but as the quiet compass guiding life toward purpose and balance. It's not about chasing happiness but about finding that intersection where passion (*suki*), mission (*tokui*), vocation (*shigoto*), and profession converge — a sweet spot where meaning resides (*seikatsu no hitsuyou*).

Ikigai transforms the ordinary into the extraordinary, infusing each day with direction and calm. It doesn't promise easy answers but offers resilience in hardship, joy in simplicity, and a way of living that aligns with the rhythms of life itself. Like a thread weaving through existence, ikigai connects the self to the greater whole, showing that fulfillment isn't found in what you achieve but in the way you live.

GRANDPARENTS

In 2018, our older daughter, Danielle, gave birth to our first grandchild, Cameron. This was an event that tilted the decision to repatriate. We wanted to have a close relationship with our grandchildren, and we knew a close relationship required regular interaction: We needed to be in the same country!

I thought I was too young to be a grandfather. I was only 58 years old. But Cameron was so much fun, he made being a grandfather easy. Cameron exhibits genuine affection for "Earl" and "Lissa", which made me grateful.

About two years later, Danielle and Brendan had their second son, Jackson. Jackson is a fun kid. He is very animated and shows great enthusiasm for Melissa and me. He's a joy to be around.

In 2024, Madison and Brendan had their first child, Colin Arthur Davies. Colin's middle name was in honor of my father, which almost brought me to tears.

Our entire family was now on a development journey.

As for how this affects my journey, I can say Cameron, Jackson, and Colin [2] bring me joy. They make me a happier, kinder, and more thoughtful person.

Seeing Lissa enjoying the grandkids, and the grandkids enjoying her, is heartwarming too.

---

[2] and maybe more to come…

IKIGAI AND MY ENCORE YEARS

After The Second Mountain was published, David Brooks wrote an article in The Atlantic entitled The New Old Age. It was a great follow-up to The Second Mountain. The article was about action. He wrote about what people and learning institutions are doing to help people develop a Second Mountain plan. He came up with a synonym for the Second Mountain — the Encore Years — the term I use.

The basic message in the article is that most people don't know where to start. Upon reflection, I thought about all this work I've done. I decided to write my vision and mission statement for my Encore Years.

It turned out that my Encore Years required ikigai. On one day I would be thinking, "What is my Second Mountain". On another day, I would be thinking, "What's my purpose, my ikigai?" Day after day of compartmentalized thinking led me to an epiphany — they are connected. One isn't a path and the other a purpose. The purpose is the path, and the path is the purpose. With that, things just clicked.

My Encore Years Ikigai

1. Serve My Family

Be a loving husband. Be a meaningful father. Make a difference in my grandkid's lives. Make the time spent together with my family count. Love my family unconditionally. Savor the time spent. Make memories. Leave a positive, lasting impression. Make an impact on their lives.

2. Be in Service to My Friends

Be a good friend. Stay connected to them. Visit friends in person. Do things with them. Makes new meaningful friendships. Make the time spent together count. Savor the time spent. Make memories. Leave a positive, lasting impression. Make an impact on their lives.

3. Help Friends Transition into Their Encore Years

Share with friends what I've learned about moving into my Encore Years. Give them materials to aid their transition. Talk to them often. Be a listener. Be joyed by their discovery. Refine my process of helping.

4. Serve My Community

Maintain a men's club to promote a kindred spirit, emotionally, physically, and spiritually. Have dinners centered around discussing either the Encore Years, or the world's beauty, or serving the needs of others.

5. Serve Myself

   a. Serve Myself I: Pursue Activities I Love

   Flyfish. Hike. Travel. Go on adventures. Immerse myself in the experience. Elevate my skill. Savor the moment.

Experience the joy of where I am. Share the experience with others.

    b.   Serve Myself II: Take Care of My Body

Eat good food. Don't overeat. Exercise. Maintain a healthy weight. Meditate. Get checked regularly.

    c.   Serve Myself III: Have a Strong Sense of Spirituality
Nature is my temple. Experience Awe. Be compassionate and kind. Ponder unknowns. Marvel at the miracle and complexity of life.

    d.   Serve Myself IV: Make Art

Take photographs. Draw. Tie flies.

6. Be an Ambassador for Beauty

Highlight the beauty in nature, the beauty in people, and the beauty in culture. Show or share it with people. Tell stories about it.

7. Keep My Passion for Investing Alive

    a.   Build a Sustainable Income Portfolio

Evaluate market returns and make sure my investments are providing their most attractive returns. Do the research, maximize returns, manage the risk, minimize tax.

    b.   Build a Growth Portfolio

Read the research. Analyze things. Stay curious. Invest. Involve others and listen to their points of view. Enjoy the feeling (intellectually and financially) of getting it right. Learn from getting it wrong.

LOOKING FORWARD

In the book Chasing Daylight, Eugene O'Kelly doesn't talk about time the way most people do. He doesn't treat it like a clock, something measured in numbers and deadlines. He breaks it into moments — sharp, defined, intentional. Not just experiences that happen, but experiences that are crafted, deliberately shaped before they slip away. When he learns he has only a few months to live, time stops being an abstraction. It becomes something real, something finite, something to be handled with precision, not wasted in the usual unconscious drift.

The way O'Kelly describes moments is different from the way most people live. Most just accumulate time passively, letting it wash over them without distinction. They assume there will always be more, so they don't bother to frame anything clearly. But when O'Kelly knows the end is near, every encounter, every conversation, every sunset becomes something to be closed, completed in a way that leaves no loose ends. He doesn't just spend time with people — he creates a moment with them, elevates it, makes it something that can stand alone, fully formed, so that when it's gone, it doesn't feel unfinished.

That's how I will spend my life. It's my Second Mountain Zeitgeist. Zeitgeist is a German word that translates to "spirit of the times." But unlike its broad use referring to the defining ideas, beliefs, and cultural atmosphere of a particular period in history, it's defining my beliefs and attitudes moving forward.

Life isn't a seamless, continuous flow. It's a series of well-shaped events — or at least, it should be. Most people live under the illusion that life will always keep stretching forward, that they'll have more time to make sense of things. But when the countdown is real, when you can see the exact number of days left, there's no room for illusion anymore. You either give each moment its full weight, or you let it pass, half-lived, into the blur of time that nobody remembers.

Why wait until time is running out to truly live? Why not shape moments now, instead of just letting them happen?

APPENDIX

PHOTOGRAPHS

1973. My Bar Mitzvah: L to R: Arthur, Grandma Eve, Debbie, Me, Grandma Essie, Lois

1982. Senior College Photo Washington University in St. Louis

1965. 5 years old, Riverdale, Bronx, New York

1978. Senior Class Photo, Harrison, NY

April 26, 1986. Our Wedding Day, St. Louis, Missouri

1995. Danielle and Madison, St. Louis, Missouri

PHOTOGRAPHS 63

2015. Corvatch, Canton Graubünden, Switzerland

2015. Chäserrugg, Churfirsten, Canton St. Gallen

2016. Melissa with Wildflowers, Eggberge, Canton Ur

64   SEARCHING

2009. Ryoanji Temple, Kyoto, Japan

2004. Park City, Utah

PHOTOGRAPHS

2002. Sockeye Salmon, Prince of Wales Island, Alaska

2024, Patagonia, Chile

2005. Melissa, Me, Danielle, Madison. Hotaka, Japan

2023. Oyunohara Torii, Hongu, Japan

PHOTOGRAPHS 67

2023. Kumano Hongu Taisha, Hongu, Japan

2023. Daimonzaka, Kumano Kodo, Nachi, Japan

2018. Seeing Cameron for the first time. Zürich, Switzerland

2019. Cameron and me, Washington University in St. Louis

2023, Jackson and me, Johns Island, SC

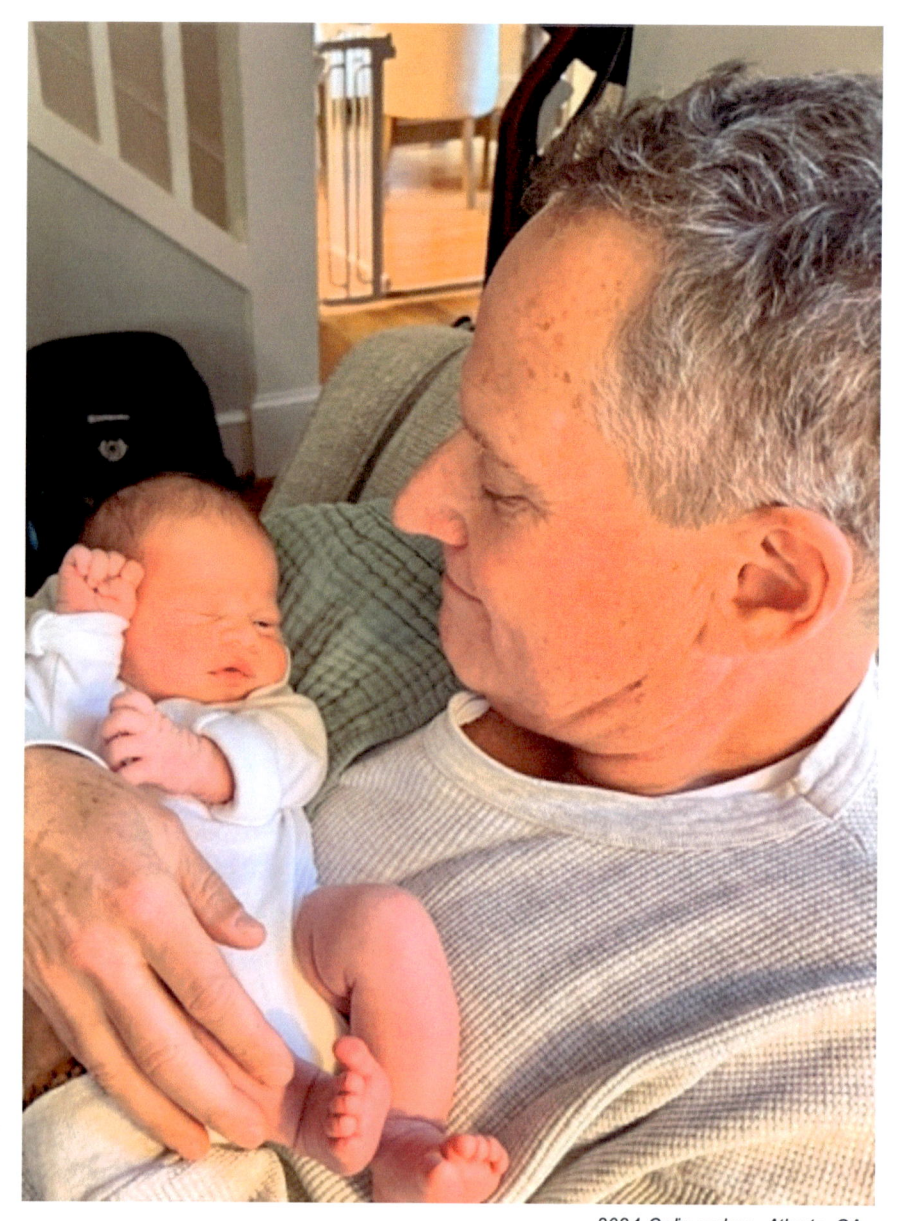

2024. Colin and me. Atlanta, GA

ACKNOWLEDGMENTS

Writing this book presented some challenges. The goal was clear: Share my mental model for living life. But I was unsure if the kaleidoscope of thoughts would make sense to the reader.

I also wondered, "Would anyone care about my story?" I quickly let that though go, for I believe the art of letting go is the art of living. Living our best life requires courage to release what no longer serves us, wisdom to trust the flow of life, and the embrace of beauty that lies ahead.

… and so, it began.

This journey would not have been possible without the insights and wisdom of the authors and thinkers whose works have inspired this book. All referenced books are in the bibliography.

I am forever grateful to Melissa. She has shown unwavering support for me and my journey. Honey, everyplace we have gone, and everything we have done, has its place. They all happened for a reason, and I am beginning to understand why.

My father once said to me, you give your children only three things: your unconditional love, an education, and memories. To Danielle and Madison, writing this book for you reflects all three. It has only gotten better with your two Brendans, and your children.

When my grandmother died, she had a book and a New York Times article clipping on her nightstand. The book was written by my great grandfather, Abraham Gallant. I didn't know anything about him. The foreword in the book was written by my great uncle, Joe Gallant. It was a eulogy, detailing his life. Abraham Gallant prepared the book for printing the night of his fatal operation for cancer. The newspaper article was about him too. It detailed how thousands of people from the community, trying to show their last respects for this great man, turned into a riot.

This book was inspired by the feelings I had reading that foreword and news article about my great grandfather. I kept thinking, "I didn't know anything about him". So, for my grandchildren: Cameron, Jackson, Colin, and hopefully more to come, I write this for you.

I am grateful to so many friends who took time to talk about these topics over the years. I talked most often with Greg McGreevey. He remains my co-pilot on this metaphysical journey. I also spoke often with Dave Semel and Gib Webb, two guys who went deep on many topics. Andy Selig was instrumental in my self-discovery. I learned a lot from him. He was a role model.

I'm grateful for the insights from John Gattuso, Howard Handler, Clint Kisker, Sean Kisker, Patrick Litré, Edward Mills, Paul Mellinger, Dan Saltzstein, Mitch Semel, Antoine Shettritt, Jeff Trenton, Gerald Wigger, Bill Winkelmann, and Dieter Wirth. You guys each offered a beacon of light on these topics.

In Serenbe I was blessed with a men's group that delved into these topics: I cherished my time with Dave Gallagher, Scott Lindsey, Marc Schwartz, Brandan Murphy, Tom Reed, and Rusty Zarse.

Most notably, I am forever grateful to Philipp Wagner. Sarai per sempre il signor Simpatico. Everything we have done together epitomizes the topics in this book.

BIBLIOGRAPHY

Covey, Stephen R. *The Seven Habits of Highly Effective People: Powerful Lessons in Personal Change.* Free Press, 1989.

Csikszentmihalyi, Mihaly. *Flow: The Psychology of Optimal Experience.* Harper & Row, 1990.

Dalai Lama, and Howard C. Cutler. *The Art of Happiness: A Handbook for Living.* Riverhead Books, 1998.

Duncan, David James. *The River Why.* Sierra Club Books, 1983.

Ford, Debbie. *The Dark Side of the Light Chasers: Reclaiming Your Power, Creativity, Brilliance, and Dreams.* Riverhead Books, 1998.

García, Héctor, and Francesc Miralles. *Ikigai: The Japanese Secret to a Long and Happy Life.* Penguin Books, 2016.

O'Kelly, Eugene, with Andrew Postman. *Chasing Daylight: How My Forthcoming Death Transformed My Life.* McGraw-Hill, 2006.

Pirsig, Robert M. Lila: *An Inquiry into Morals.* Bantam Books, 1991.

Pirsig, Robert M. *Zen and the Art of Motorcycle Maintenance: An Inquiry into Values.* William Morrow,

1974.

Ruiz, Don Miguel Ángel. *The Four Agreements: A Practical Guide to Personal Freedom.* Amber-Allen Publishing, 1997.

Seligman, Martin E. P. *Authentic Happiness: Using the New Positive Psychology to Realize Your Potential for Lasting Fulfillment.* Free Press, 2002.

Suzuki, Daisetz Teitaro. *Introduction to Zen Buddhism.* Foreword by C.G. Jung. New York: Grove Press, 1964.

Wilson, Edward O. The Social Conquest of Earth. Liveright Publishing, 2012.

OTHER READINGS

Brooks, Arthur C. *"Your Professional Decline Is Coming (Much) Sooner Than You Think."* The Atlantic, July 2019, www.theatlantic.com.

Brooks, Arthur C. *"The Happy Art of Grandparenting."* The Atlantic, June 22, 2023, www.theatlantic.com.

Brooks, David. *"The New Old Age."* The Atlantic, May 2023, www.theatlantic.com.

Hill, Faith. *"The Curious Personality Changes of Old Age."* The Atlantic, July 2023, www.theatlantic.com.

Rilke, Rainer Maria. *Letters to a Young Poet.* Tranlated by M. D. Herter Norton, W. W. Norton & Company, 1934.

EXERCISES

1. 生きがい　Ikigai

The word *ikigai* is the combination of 生き (*iki* — "life" or "living") and がい (*gai* — "worth" or "value"). Together, ikigai means "reason for being" or "purpose in life." Answers the following questions to identify your ikigai. What do you love? What are you good at? What does the world need? What can you be paid for?

2. 一期一会　Ichigo ichie

Ichigo ichie can be translated as "treasure every moment as a once-in-a-lifetime experience." The practice of ichigo ichie cultivates mindfulness by encouraging full presence in each moment, treating every encounter as unique and unrepeatable. This mindset deepens relationships, enhances appreciation for daily experiences, and reduces stress by shifting focus away from past regrets or future anxieties. In Japanese culture, it is a reminder to embrace the beauty of the present with gratitude and awareness.

3. 森林浴　Shinrin-yoku

Shinrin-yoku refers to the practice of immersing oneself in nature, particularly in forests, to promote relaxation and well-being. It is a well-known concept in Japanese wellness culture, emphasizing the healing effects of spending mindful time in the forest. As you walk, focus on the sights, sounds, and sensations around you. Reflect on how being present transforms the experience.

4. 感謝　Kansha

Kansha can be interpreted as "gratitude". Practicing kansha shifts your focus from what is lacking to what is abundant, fostering a deeper sense of contentment and fulfillment. It strengthens relationships, enhances mental well-being, and cultivates resilience by encouraging mindfulness of the present moment. In Japanese culture, expressing gratitude is seen as a key element of living a meaningful and harmonious life.

5.   居場所 Ibasho

Ibasho means "a place where one belongs" or "a sense of connection within a community." Having an ibasho provides emotional security, social support, and a deep sense of belonging. It fosters meaningful relationships, reduces stress, and enhances overall well-being by reinforcing a shared purpose. In Japanese culture, people with a strong ibasho often experience greater happiness and longevity, as they feel valued and connected to others in a supportive environment.

Image: Back Cover, Ikigai: The Japanese Secret to a Long and Happy Life

Made in the USA
Columbia, SC
28 February 2025